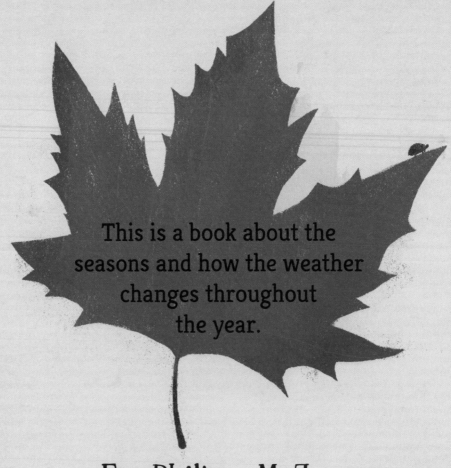

This is a book about the
seasons and how the weather
changes throughout
the year.

For Philip – M. J.

For Edward – R. J.

First published 2018 by Walker Books Ltd 87 Vauxhall Walk, London SE11 5HJ

2 4 6 8 10 9 7 5 3 1

Text © 2017 Martin Jenkins

Illustrations © 2017 Richard Jones

The right of Martin Jenkins and Richard Jones to be identified as author and illustrator respectively of this work
has been asserted by them in accordance with the Copyright, Designs and Patents Act 1988

This book has been typeset in Kreon
Printed in China

British Library Cataloguing in Publication Data: a catalogue record for this book is available from the British Library

ISBN 978-1-4063-5514-7

www.walker.co.uk

WALKER BOOKS
AND SUBSIDIARIES
LONDON · BOSTON · SYDNEY · AUCKLAND

The Squirrels' Busy Year

Martin Jenkins

Illustrated by
Richard Jones

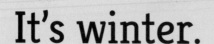

It's winter.

It's cold! The sun is low in the sky, the pond is frozen over and there's snow on the ground. It's very quiet. In a hole in the trunk of the big tree perches an owl, keeping an eye on things.

When it's cold, water freezes and turns to ice.

The sun makes the heat that warms the world. It warms us more when it's high in the sky than when it's low down. The sun is never very high in the sky in winter.

Not too far away, two squirrels are curled up in their cosy nest. They can't stay there for ever, though. They'll soon get hungry and then they'll need to go out and find something to eat.

They'd better get a move on. It will soon be dark.

Down the trunk.
Over by the stump…
A quick dig and yes!
Some acorns.

In winter, the days are short
and the nights are long.

It's snowing again.
Time to get back to the nest.

Snow comes from water in clouds. It needs to be cold for snow to fall.

It's spring.

It's warm. The ice and snow have all gone. It's noisy! There are birds singing in the bushes and the pond is full of frogs, croaking fit to burst. Not all the birds are making a noise. In the hole in the big tree the owl is sitting quietly, keeping an eye on things.

When it's warm, snow and ice melt and turn into water.

The sun is higher in the sky during
the day in spring than in winter.

The squirrels are out and about, looking for food.

The acorns are all gone, but there are
fat, juicy buds on the maple trees.

Maple trees lose their leaves in winter and grow new ones each spring.
The buds that the squirrels don't eat will turn into leaves.

The sun is setting, but the squirrels are still busy.

Now they're digging up bulbs.

Whoosh!

That was close!

It's summer.

It's hot. The frogs are keeping cool in the pond.
It's quiet and still. The squirrels are lazing about,
staying out of the sun. And up in the big tree,
in his hole in the trunk, sits
the owl.

The days are long in summer
and in the middle of the day
the sun is very high in the sky.

The clouds are getting bigger.
The sky is darkening and
there's a wind blowing.

Rumble rumble.

What was that?

The rumble is thunder. Thunderstorms mostly happen in the summer.

Rumble rumble. Crack!

Goodness – the big tree. It's on fire!

Did the owl get away?

Rain, thunder and lightning all come from clouds.

It's autumn.

It's a bit chilly. The frogs have disappeared, but they haven't gone far: they're sleeping in the mud at the bottom of the pond.

Autumn days are shorter than summer days and the sun is
not as high in the sky in the middle of the day.

Most of the birds have flown off somewhere warmer.
Some of them are still around, though.

The weather is often cool in autumn and it can be wet and windy.
The birds that have flown off will come back in the spring.
Many trees lose their leaves in autumn.

The squirrels are busy
picking up acorns.

Every now and then
they eat one or two ...

but mostly they just
carry them off, one after
another after another, and
bury them in the ground.

Because in a few weeks' time it will be winter and there might be snow. Most of the time the squirrels will be tucked up in their nest ... but every now and again they'll have to go out and find something to eat.

THINKING ABOUT
SEASONS AND WEATHER

What time of year is it where you are?
How many kinds of plants can you see growing nearby?
How many of them have flowers? How many have leaves?
How do you think your answers will be different
in six months' time?

INDEX

Look up the pages to find out about seasons and weather. Don't forget to look up both kinds of word, this kind - and **this kind.**

BIBLIOGRAPHY

Here are some other Science Storybooks.

Fox in the Night by Martin Jenkins,
Walker Books (2017)

Bird Builds a Nest by Martin Jenkins,
Walker Books (2018)